D1288864

Note to the readers:

The intention of this publication is to offer useful and informative material about the topic it addresses. The strategies pointed out in this book may not be appropriate for every reader and there is no guarantee that the expected result of applying the learnings of this publication. Having said that, it is not know of any adverse effects of applying them to date, and it has been tested in different enviornments and with people of different social, cultural and demographic backgroune. This book is sold taking into account that neither the author, nor the editor, or the printing entity, are excusively dedicated to rendering professional legal or psychological services or of any other kind. The reader can of course address other people such as grown-ups, parents, teachers, bosses, friends and relatives, and of course physical, mental or spiritual professionals, to get support in the implementation or applicaton of the suggestions of this book or the complementary material that can be obtained throught it., although him or herself may of course draw his or her own conclusions. No guarantee is provided regarding the precision or completeness of the information provided here, although it is based in long validated social psychology theory, as well as on personal experiences and those of third parties that the author has access to. The author, the editor, the printing companies, the designer deny explicitly any responsibility for the losses or damages that any reader may incur into by reading the contents of this book Although the author would like it otherwise, for the time being, any copy, in part or in full, without the explicit and written consent of the author is forbidden.

Like a fish in water
Translated into English with the support of Alex Carver, Anthony Barrueta and Erin Meadows
© Begoña San Jose 2021
Self-publication and design by Begoña San Jose
bego@beandgo.eu

This publication is de facto subject to regular modifications, corrections, updates and clarifications on behalf of the author and the opinions exposed in it are her own.

LIKE A FISH IN WATER

The little bird who lived like a fish water

A story for the small ones to fall asleep
and for grown-ups to wake up

Begoña San José

To my husband, for loving me free and flying high.

To my children, for teaching me and inspiring me to be better everyday.

To a long list of wonderful people for accompanying me in my flights.

To Alex Carver, Anthony Barrueta and Erin Meadows for their generous contribution to fine-tuning this story into English language and context.

To the readers of this story, for sharing their own stories and for inspiring me to continuisly improve this and future editions and publications.

"If you are always trying to be normal,

you will never know how *amazing*

you can be"

Maya Angelou

Once, not too long ago, there was Pio, a little bird who lived like a fish in water.

He saw like a fish. He sang like a fish. He lived like a fish.

A little bird who felt **like a fish in water.**

It all started one day when he went looking for his place in the world. He did not like his wings so much, so he hardly ever flew. He did not like his voice so much, so he hardly ever sang.

As he walked by the water's edge, he saw his own reflection, together with some fish, right there, just under the water! The fish had the exact same colours as his own wings.

Without giving it much thought, he jumped into the water and swam away with them.

At first, he swam with a long straw. Then with fins, then with diving goggles.

He even got a neoprene suit! Not only could he swim like a fish, but he dressed like one too.

How else could he live like fish in the water?

He came out of the water to get some air, but he soon rushed back. He lived like a fish, and he felt **like a fish in water**.

He had fun like a fish, although he often got tired at parties and he did not understand the lyrics of the songs with so many bubbles...

With his oxygen tank on his back, he never needed to leave the water.

In the water he had, all that he needed.

He even found a cave, where he could take the heavy oxygen tank off his back and sing freely.

The fish that occasionally heard him sing gave him a funny look, because when they opened their "beaks", only bubbles came out.

It was not long before he stopped singing at all.

He really lived **like a fish in water**.

Well, maybe not so much.

Some days, the oxygen tank felt heavy on his shoulders. Every once in a while, he would swim up to the surface.

The diving googles fogged up whenever he left the water. As he was leaning by the waterside, he saw his own reflection, but Pio did not recognize himself. So, he rushed back into the water and continued swimming *in his own world*.

More and more, the oxygen tank felt heavier and heavier - he often found it difficult to go about his day-to-day life.

He would go out with friends, but he hardly opened his beak. He would go to parties, but he wouldn't say a word, hiding behind a rock.

He started to think that the other fish could not even see him.

Maybe his neoprene suit made him invisible?

One evening up at the surface, he saw the flash of a lighthouse beam far in the distance, and he heard a bird singing.

He tried to reply with his own song, but nothing came out.

How on earth could he sing with that snorkel on his beak?

Luckily, that other bird got up the courage to fly by.
With a couple of pecks, he got rid of his new friend's foggy
diving googles.

Perched by the waterside, Pio saw his own reflection. It
seemed clearer now, without the foggy googles, but he did not
recognize himself.

Pio rushed back into the water.

But, under water, without the diving googles, his eyes were itching and he was crying; He was not sure if his eyes were itching because he was crying, or if he was crying because his eyes were itching. But, quietly and alone, he was crying.

The fish did not understand anything. What could they possibly know about diving googles? -They just laughed-.

They started to think he was going crazy... or was he really going crazy?

He sank into sadness. The oxygen tank on his shoulders was heavier and heavier and he felt he was going deeper and deeper, down into the water where he couldn't even see the beam of that lighthouse far away on the surface.

Well and truly fed up, one day Pio took the oxygen tank off his own back and swam to the surface.

It's better this way, he thought. Lighter.

He tried to sing but it was all out of tune. So long since he last sang!

He tried to fly but he could only shake the water off his wings. So long since he last used them!

The other birds could sing beautifully, and they could also fly and they had bright, beautiful coloured feathers!

How could he possibly fly with that neoprene suit of his?

Was it really a good idea to jump out of the water?

Without the oxygen tank, without the diving googles, over the surface of the water, he saw his own reflection, together with one other bird next to him.

He recognized himself! and he saw that he somehow looked like the other birds too.

Some of those birds -with gentle pecks- helped him get rid of his neoprene skin and reveal his own feathers.

Although he, himself, he felt ashamed, naked.

Every day, he listened to the other birds singing and he watched them fly.

His own feathers slowly recovered their colours and his voice became stronger and stronger, more confident with every song.

His wings, so free from the weight of the water, were also getting stronger.

One day, helped by the wind, he flew off the branch.

At the beginning there were short, tiring flights barely off the ground. Soon the flights got longer and longer, higher and higher, up in the bright blue sky.

He crashed against trees and branches a thousand times. Sometimes as he opened his beak, bubbles would come out.

Once -or maybe twice- he thought he saw little fish in nests around him.

Sometimes he felt out of breath, after so many years of re-lying on the oxygen tank.

He slowly left behind those days clinging terrified to the branch of a tree, when it shook and cracked on stormy days. His own soul shook too – absolutely terrified!

But slowly, very slowly, as he practiced being Pio, flight after flight, crash after crash, he proved himself able to make beautiful pirouettes and loops, singing joyful operettas.

He learned children's songs that the younger birds repeated. The younger ones listened carefully to the stories of the lives of the fish.

They understood, clearer than water, that flying was more fun. Wearing neoprene and feeling heavy all day was more a fish costume.

And almost even more fun than flying was another way to use a straw- not to breath air from beneath the water, but to blow endless bubbles in the water!

And even more fun than blowing endless bubbles is to fly really high! So hight that your wings do not get wet from the splashes of water the fish sometimes make while swimming **like fish in water**.

Every sunset, just before the sun goes away, when the whole place is covered by that golden powder, we can all see Pio flying high.

Wings spread wide, in a flying exhibition, making amazing patterns in the clouds.

And just before landing, he performs one last flight across the water, singing and laughing as loud as he can, just in case there's another bird down there, swimming **like a fish in water**.

That's it!

Like a fish, but **without being a fish**.

Sometimes in fairy tales and stories alike a comma makes a difference and changes the meaning of a sentence completely. Sometimes, instead of a comma, it is a "like".

And if you want to know what happened to the fish, you will have to go and ask them yourself... but we all know they only have the memory of fish.

This story, like yours, is not over.
It goes on and on – it has only just begun.

"If you judge a fish for its ability to climb trees, it will live its whole life be-lieveing that it is stupid"

Albert Einstein

Questions to reflect upon
LIKE FISH IN THE WATER Begoña San José

1. Do you identify yourself with Pio, do you live like fish in the water without being a fish? Do you feel sometimes like an alien just landed from a different planet?

2. Are you aware of the small efforts you make to be like the others, to adapt, to be just one more?

3. Do you have experience breathing through a long strow? Have you had experience with the whole equipment, oxygen bottle included?

4. Do you believe you have everything you need under water? Have you found yourself a cave, a safe-space where you can sing and be yourself?

5. Have you stopped singing, have you stopped doing something that you considered part of your true self, of your essence, in order to fit in an environment, maybe at school, at the office, at home, in whatever country you may live?

6. Do you feel or have you felt the weight of the oxygen bottle in your back? Do you feel or have you felt you were becoming transparent, invisible? Do you feel or have you felt that you were drawining? Have you felt what I call "psychological asfixia"?

7. Have you seen other birds and the light of the lighthouse back in the surface? Has any little or big bird come by you to help you get rid of your googles?

8. Have you got to thinking that you would not be able to fly again, that you would not be able to sing again? Have you felt ashamed, naked? Have you wondered if you did the right thing by getting out of the water?

9. Do yo feel or have you felt tired after your first short flights? Have you seen bubbles when you opened your beak? Have you felt out of breath, or maybe clinging terrified to the branch of a tree on stormy days? Have you crashed against trees and branches?

10. Have you managed to make beautiful pirouettes and sing operetas? Have you talked to others about the feeling of wearing a fish custume? Do you fill the water with endless bubbles from out-side? Do you fly with your wings spread wide, in a flying exhi-bition?

And now what?
I know, by my own experience, that you would be thinking
that it is easier to say than to actually bring into practice...
and for that reason, I have also created:

"Tips to be yourself"
and I offer courses and group workshops

If you are interested in getting these tips, or in receiving
more information about the courses and workshops, the only
thing you have to do is to write me a message on email,
or on Instagram or Facebook:

comopezenelagua@beandgo.eu

@bego.beandgo o "be and go":

If you found this story useful, I would really appreciate you
get back to me now to tell me
How did you find this story? Or
How did this sroty find you, instead?

If while reading this story, you thought of someone,
Why don't you give it as a present?
My initial plan was to give everyone for each purchase of this
story, a second one, but that is not very feasible for the
time being. However, you can do it yourself, and add your own
message to the person too, in the blanc spaces that I have
left for that purpose.

As I have already told you, this story has only just started
and goes on, every day, with pictures and quotes that inspire
myself and others. Do you want to join us?
@bego.beandgo

In the following pages you will find the characters of this story that you can cut out if they help you identify yourself and others with them.

If you would rather have them sent by me, write me a message and I would be happy to send you a pdf file.